The Latitude
Of
Naples

0

Eva Bourke

o

The Dedalus Press — 13 Moyclare Road
Baldoyle — Dublin 13
Ireland

ISBN 1 904556 29 9 (paper)
ISBN 1 904556 30 2 (bound)

Acknowledgements:
The Recorder (Vassar College), The SHOp, Poetry Ireland Review,
Céide, Waxwing Poems, 80mph - Festschrift for Leland Bardwell,
Denkbilder - Festschrift for Eoin Bourke.
"Sonata for the Painter's Shadow" was commissioned by Brian Bourke
for the catalogue of and to accompany his exhibition entitled *Women
Giving Birth to Men*.

Cover illustration detail from painting by Benjamin de Burca.
Design Miriam de Burca

Dedalus Press books are represented and distributed in the
U.S.A. and Canada by Dufour Editions Ltd., P.O. Box 7,
Chester Springs, Pennsylvania 19425
and in the U.K. by Central Books, 99 Wallis Road, London E9
5LN

The Dedalus Press receives financial assistance
from An Chomhairle Ealaíon, The Arts Council,
Ireland

Printed in Dublin by Johnswood Press.

Contents

Magician, spread out your instruments.

Czeslaw Milosz

Wind. And the blackbirds. And the rustling of leaves
In the old black icy springs. . .

In the old black icy springs the entire water surface

Trembles now and again without any discernible reason.
And it so happens that on days like these the lesser gods

are awake.

Lars Gustafsson

FROM AHAB'S LOG BOOK

February 2002

For T. Michael Sullivan

For weeks the sea lay dozing like a cat
but three nights ago it turned over
shook its mane and rose up hissing
along the foreshore of Black Head.

Somewhere lost within its belly
tumbles my white whale,
small and luminous as a firefly.
I sailed into this westernmost town

at the dark edge of Europe
to shelter from the never-ending gales,
moored the *Pequod*
alongside a wrecked stone pier

and limped into the centre
of what seems to be a place
entirely preoccupied with holiness –
church spires, bells and convents everywhere

and since it was Ash Wednesday
the foreheads of the entire populace
were streaked with grey.
Their drink is the colour and smell of soutanes

which must be some local
form of penance,
all streets have saints' names
and no doubt lead straight to heaven.

I bide my time in a sandwich bar
beside the tackle shop
and listen to a street musician strain
the mournful air through harp strings.

Having found a companion
in a wild-haired old man, a sailor
who claims to have lost his ship and crew
somewhere in the mountains of Armenia,

we solve riddles together, anagrams,
I ask him what kept Ishmael afloat
after the *Pequod* sank:
a coffin, a barrel of oil, a lifeboat, a mattress?

He asks me what I saw
in the gold doubloon I nailed to the mast,
myself, God,
the face of evil?

This is how we pass the night
while the storm clatters
on its typewriter
above the hostelry roof.

The terraced houses lie in wait
linking arms.
If they abide long enough
they might witness the showdown.

All paths leading to the water
are empty,
the hours last
as never before.

I can expect little from the sky
from which darkness hangs
like a saw-toothed star,
a poem dictated to the night in a boarded-up room.

LATE AUTUMN IN VENICE
by R.M. Rilke

The city now no longer drifts like bait
which reels in all the surfaced days.
The glass palaces reverberate
more dimly to your eye. The summer sways

in gardens like a bundle of marionettes,
head-over-heels, exhausted, dead.
But from the deep, from old skeletal woods
a purpose rises as though overnight

the general of the seas had multiplied
by two the galleys in the watchful arsenal
tarring the next morning's early light

with a fleet which moving countless oars
jostles, hoists bright flags, all at once
has the great wind, radiant and fatal.

IN PRAISE OF ROUND THINGS

Not the straight line, the acute angle, the shortest distance
                                    between two points
but the roundabout way, the circle that refuses to be squared

not the box, the cube, the cell
but fruit baskets, sacks of apples, apples rolling in the grass
a secret fluttering among the branches of the privet hedge
that accompanies the weaving of nests, the nests
                                    like minuscule baskets

not the rectilinear, the tetragon,
but the consolations of cycles giving birth to new stars,
                                    new women
the blue apple earth with its hot fluid heart

not the T-square, the ruler
but magnolia buds white and waxlike springing from
                                    winter boughs
speckled eggs in round nests and the rotundity of o and omega
and the lemon's relations: the comfortable bellied pumpkins
                                    and melons

not the straightedge, the measure
but a ball rolling through the spring grass like a planet
one of nine spheroids with flattened poles orbited
                                    by a sprinkling of moons

not the high-rise, the Mies Van der Rohe rectangles
but green domes of cathedrals, of mosques tiled with
                                    lapis and jade
and populated with saints staring down wide-pupilled
                                    with ecstasy

not the cruciform, the perpendicular
but the lightshow of the planetarium above the green river
the orrery of the Great Earl and the great ear of the observatory
that's shaped like a saucer listening in on curved space

not the quadrangle, the hexahedron
but the sun's startled eye at daybreak alighting
on Osias Beert's porcelain bowls of strawberries and cherries
beside a platter of sombre brown olives

not the trunk, the casket, the locker
but the water barrel's roundness, three water barrels'
                              three roundnesses
echoing a young woman's chin and cheek
the apple's round cheek as she takes a bite
like the eclipse on Tuesday round about seven which took
                              a bite out of the moon

not the undeviating, the linear
but a clay bath from 3050 BC, its curviform rim still wet
the belly and breasts of the Willendorf goddess, forever pregnant
and smooth from being carried close to the heart and
                              taken out in times of need
the shadow on the sundial at Tarascon that comes round
                              and goes round
and the hands of all clocks that turn to the ticktock of a disc-like
                              invasive shadow

not the meter, the level, the quadrennium
but the astronomical clock at Strasbourg with its one
                              small cogwheel
on top of a system of cogwheels and pulleys
that in 28 000 years turns once imitating a circular movement
                              of the axis of the earth
and which replicates precisely the revolution of all the planets

as on each stroke of twelve the apostles circle gravely around
the cock crows three times and a little skeleton hammers
                                        on its brass gong

not the parallels, the unswerving, the foursquare
not the motor ways and roads full of Monday-morning faces *wondering*
but the boreens that go round and round through sundials
            Wend the winding way of blackberries
past the glittering minutiae of winding sea roads
and return to the manifold skies of Henry Street
to three neighbours, their faces aligned with the sun, gossiping
                                        in their doorways

not the unbending, the adamantine, the compartment
but the pond in the forest which contains every known
                                        mineral blue
and a nymph of the same colour who is rarely seen

not the unyielding, the strait-laced, the ramrod
but droplets on leaves writing their rondeaux in praise
                                        of watery notation
of the concert pitch A (440 Hz) as played by the round
                                        mouth of the oboe

in praise of the comings and goings of dances, of tides
to the kettle drum beat of the sea
the staccato of hailstones on lean-to roofs, the whole
                                        theatre in the round

in praise of seasons returning with outbursts
                                        of daffodil meadows
and of moss corners in mill races, of grey rice-paper globes
glued together by assiduous wasps, of ring forts on round islands
of bracelets and the tenacity of their individual links
of spider webs with their rigorous radius

13

in praise of Parmigianino's self-portrait, his young face
                              smiling distortedly
from a convex mirror and in praise of seven hot air balloons
which we watched in Dresden one summer day
being inflated on the banks of the Elbe and taking to the sky
                              one by one

in praise of Cezanne's blue apples, of snail shells which combine
                              elegance and strength
and in praise of the shimmering body lodged in the flesh
                              of the oyster
and growing harder and more perfect like a love
                    that remains concealed to the end

CAT WITH SILL

For Leland

The disciple of paradox invented the cat –
solipsism incarnate –

inscribed presence and absence
into her flawless design.

The cat invented the paradox of discipline:
not slip shod unlike us she strolls

through the *Spielraum* of possibilities
over-arching her night life.

Irony and green Pharaonic gold
between her eye slits

she folds herself Houdini-like into the sill
the overnight case, the desk drawer

taking up little more than 10 or 12 gills
in order to form a perfect ellipse;

your finger following the oval
of her body in repose would estimate

the sum of its distance from the two glittering irises
constant at every point.

Located sill-wise precisely between now and here
she meditates meanwhile

on the principle of immoderation
to which the tip of her tail is aerially connected

and if you could decipher her code
you would find routes of misdeeds

of gratuitous killings mapped out on her pelt
but also evidence of synoptic purpose

tracks of holy pilgrimage
a lifelong quest for bird's eye views.

If she could choose she would live
with a good companion in a blue-silled cottage

where the sea comes closer every spring
to test her *Spielraum*

her blanket wisdom
her dark streak, her nine lives.

LANDSCAPES WITH FIGURES

I

October

The hollyhock is well over eight feet tall
    a few pale yellow flowers along its stem
        are spaced at random
as though someone had hastily buttoned it up

one blossom has just opened at the top
    abandoning itself to the south wind
        it sways like a banner
a challenge to the diminishing light

starlings potter about the tip
    of the electric mast

and in next door's overgrown garden
    autumn spiders swing in their tricky webs
        their tables well-set for winter

across the road the eternal student
    has placed his director's chair
        at the heart of the terrace

he has laid down the laws of metaphysics
    beside his sandalled feet

and now attends to his mother
    whose face is held up to the sun like a greeting card

the day unwinds
    loosens rigging and sail

17

I leave the door on the latch
    its darkening will be soon

II

Horizontals

six o'clock   the mildest day yet
    the bay's wide curving deck glistens
        from a fresh application of lacquer

the morning unfolds parachute silks
        over islands and hills that shoulder green platters
          sprinkled with sheep

straining, tethered to long rails of light
    the clouds almost tear at the seams

the young Swiss writer on the pier
    who the night before took out a jew's harp and played
        the story of ice to an audience of twelve

notes down all he sees in plurals, writing
    clouds, winds, rains
        those skies and restless birds

at home in his village between mountains, he tells me
    there's no space for vision

but here the eye roams the open
    across foreshore and the flats of playing fields
        where the sun pushes its black pawns

towards the horizon
    which is in quicksilver motion
        running on in the iambic lines of water

or strung together like the carriages
    of the five thirty a.m.
        setting out across Lough Atalia

his gift of clairvoyance
    allows him to see into the heart of things

and observing the cormorants in little clusters on the rocks
    shake their wings at the town, he feels
        the trembling urgency of their semaphores

the man in the lobster boat
    out for the last haul of the year
        reads them like gospel

but the Esso ship sailing past Black Head
    to spread its slick message of oil
        has no time for omens

on the quay wall eight round-hulled hookers lie in state
    masts and furled sails packed in tightly
        beneath tarpaulins blacker than crape

III

Journey South

on the bus window the light is a fingertip birth
    still young, still learning to walk

bands of fog lift, softening gorse hedges, ragged fields
"look, a fountain", says the child beside me

as the road twists south, the sun with rising confidence
    dances from right to left and left to right

jazzes it up above the bus roof
    now and again alighting on the passengers' heads

all of them women, who, dozing or in mid-sentence
    stretch and feel an indefinable sense of blessing

the driver steers as though conducting
    the non-stop plainsong of chat behind him

whenever he opens the door
    the air comes in, sippable as whiskey

the mist's white script is legible for a moment
    between alder branches, a book opening on stillness

we grow lighter, my love, as we grow older
    less impermeable to what is unspoken

to writings without alphabet, our hair like thistledown
    through which darkness now and again runs its fingers

LITTLE ISLAND

For John

I

Place of Drunkenness

Try getting lost here. The gleaming horizons
are piled on top of each other and clouds
are blown through streets at fiftieth floor level.
All day we were walking in circles and found ourselves
back again every time on the world's
straightest avenue along the spine of Little Island.
It led us from red light to red light,
each souvenir shop was choc-a-bloc with disaster.

In pubs full of sour smoke we fell in with men
in check shirts, broad as Atlases, their faces softened
by flickering screens. Rain kept on falling,
drove us into the church of exiles,
they slept on long benches in nests of rubbish.
We could only guess what epiphanies took place
in this temple. Next to it on a sky-high treasury
a golden eagle dug his talons deep into the globe.

The entire world was on wheels by the river —
speed being the day's second buzzword — young men
rolled past on their blades, but we, knowing no better
strolled like flâneurs who have no home to go to.
A chorus line of black graduates marched into a hall
to the sound of brass as we retraced our steps,
their heels clacked with the purposeful
choreography of initiation.

We balanced along the abyss of ourselves
lost in visions of love restored to the city

21

which lay like a great wounded beast in the rain.
From multi-media façades a kitsch alphabet was washed
onto the tarmac and crossed out by taxis.
Further down where the buildings grew more distant
and haughty, their arsenals more highly polished,
the park was leafing through its green cover story.

My companion said there was a correlation
between his sadness and the water that fell from the sky.
Poems were inscribed in the lines of his witty kind face.
Our exhaustion became so immense we could hardly lift
our eyes to the heights which were shrouded
by shimmering bands of mist,
an art nouveau pine comb swam like a mirage   *PINE CONE ?*
above the roof tops of the city.

We wandered, caught in a Pollock canvas whose colours
kept running until in the blue hour we found refuge
with Mexicans who poured us luminous mixes, green cocktails
in tall glasses. We licked every last drop from our fingers,
listened to the till singing until time was called.
Rain episodes and sirens had diverted us
into the arms of dissolution. Fat angels in navy
warned us to be vigilant. In a side street we saw

a dark Narcissus deconstruct mirrors. The clownishness
of the gesture was not lost on us. Wordless
we turned north haunted by a drama of cafés and subways,
abandoned umbrellas and movie houses,
the city humming the score of a minimalist composition—
from Finland perhaps. Drunkenness shortened
the long way home. In the end it was the rain,
we supposed, which had put all the colours to sleep.

II

Village Blues

How the monuments have outgrown
this unkempt little centre city green
playing to a gallery that doesn't pay the slightest attention,

even if it gives itself airs with triumphal
arches and the relic of a fountain
whose basin is just a bowl of dust *au fond*,

and despite cool make-overs in late
fall when the sky glints like Mrs Schneeflock's hair-net
grey on white with a sprinkling of miniature beads,

it will always be a frayed patch of grass,
suffering from a bad dose of shrinkage,
around which apartment blocks are stacked high like shoe boxes.

Oh, the days of white flights
of steps leading down to richer green shade
lawns like velours beneath rostrums of trees.

Henry James' grandchildren,
a tarnished but enduring *jeunesse dorée*,
assemble in George's Dog Run,

relax and unleash their golden darlings.
Engrossed in dog owner problems
they recommend braces for overbite,

contact lenses for aging collies,
Prozak against melancholy, remedies
for thyroid conditions and loneliness

while the eponymous George looks a little crest-
fallen on his pedestal. (Perhaps he feels
it's the unbreakable-as-Bessemer steel

energy and genius of a man like A.L. Holley
what's needed in America
these bad sad days?)

Where patriot turned candlemaker comes upon
Antonio Mencci, inventor of the telephone,
(a man much-neglected in the encyclopaedias),

I join a dreamer on a park bench
to read *The Manifesto of Capitalism,* just purchased
outside the Silver Centre of the A. and S.

from the author, Mr Solomon, for 10 dollars—
a thoroughgoing analysis
of the *Wealth of Nations* by Adam Smith

but I'm distracted by the man next to me:
*I'm turning on the volume on my desire
to soar,* he says, scanning the beat on his knee.

The lions flanking the steps like *cordons
insanitaires* to Frank J. Tasco's
and his wife Edwardine's brownstone

drop their superannuated guardian demon's air
calling *laissez faire, laissez faire*
through broken stone teeth.

They have been grazing on city dust too long
to flaunt their arsenals of destruction
and would give anything

to be released and lope across
for a rest in the shade of the acacia trees.
The song of the village chanteuse

walking past me with her glittering array
of plastic bags has a refrain which goes:
earth is darker than space

which is undeniably so, but the young woman called Bea
I see later that day in Starbuck's on 5th Avenue
as she stares into her Apple, sips iced tea

and chats with boyfriend Dan on her cell phone
will, I hope, be kept by her soul's innocence
and all benign forces forever from singing this blues.

MIDI
for Rachel and Fiacc

I

Summer with quote by Immanuel K.

The way yellow lines turn white, the further you travel, and cities
from green to blue and uniforms from blue to green, the way
coins grow weightier and sprout ears of corn, bitter coffee be-
comes sweet foam in your mouth and your own name is a for-
gotten childhood name, the way a flock of geese passes overhead
with the affirmative music of their wings, *andante cantabile,* the
way the light falls across sunflower fields and flashes back from
the sunlit canal playing with the mirror image of a double row of
plane trees in all their various greens and you're transported into
a playing card world where the stakes are no deeper than water,
the way men wear silver talismans on their chests and you're cer-
tain heart is trumps, and although you don't understand the lan-
guage you hear the petrol station attendant say *the world is a vast
playground of variety, order, function and beauty to our speechless and elo-
quent amazement,* and the way the other young man pockets his
change and drives off in his small red Renault *con moto* giving a
short wave of assent

II

Walled city

We follow fig tree lanes uphill to the walled city whose ramparts
now belong to a local lizard. It looks like a mossed-over stick
except for the pale rice paper skin of its underbelly and sides
through which the tremors of the little heart can be seen. The
castle ingress towers above a carousel jingling tunes while the
whole circus of colonial whimsey – ostriches, leopards, camels –
marches round and round against the clock. A man has been

pouring lubricant into the works from a long-spouted can. Now
he mounts the platform to assist the children on their dizzy revo-
lutions. Nymphs with bare plaster breasts hold up the baldachin
constantly turning, and with them turn stucco clowns, silk roses,
the moon, and the reedy harmonium crooning solemnly off-key
everybody loves somebody sometime... Come nightfall the walled city
and its towers fill with light and float out high above the dark
wilderness of the plain. One family is left behind on the shut-
tered fairground posing for snaps as the father takes careful aim.

III

Locks

So close to the Pyrennees the setting sun is maître de plaisir and
all around defer to him. The canal obediently reflects the upside
down lock keeper on his red bicycle flying at top speed over the
bridge just as our boat vanishes in the darkness beneath it. We've
all become part of a green and golden protocol. Spiders leave
their gauze wheels between umbrella pine branches and venture
into headlong falls, unfastened at last from the terrible ethic of
their labour. A patrol of black dragonflies emerge from the reeds
to erase the mosquitoes scribbling away above the water surface.
All day we have been climbing uphill from lock to lock until we
reached the summit which is almost equidistant from two seas,
one to the North, wild and cold – the other, our destination,
calm blue and southerly. Afloat between two dark gates we are
not even a crease in the fabric of the evening. Now the lock
keeper, who balances crane-like on a slender rusty catwalk, opens
sluice after sluice and the water hangs its heavy green glass sheet
into the lower basin. We sink to the undersong of the spillway
until the iron wings clank open trailing their wet hems of nettles
and cinquefoil. On both banks the plane trees stand aside a little
to let us pass. Their parallel shadows stream back towards the
last lock, towards the night, which comes silently, its pockets
filled with darkness and with sleep.

CORSETS, JITTERBUG AND FEET

I

My very small aunts wore corsets
all their lives, wire hoops to support
spines that listed. Embracing them was like hugging a bird

cage; heads weighed down with beak-like noses
a mild expression in their eyes
they fluttered up and down the house

in the black habits and starched white nurse's caps
I never saw them without until their death
or they'd alight on a chair like magpies

their feet not quite touching the ground
they nodded off the moment they sat down.
Never idle, always on the look-out for a torn

button or sock they unrolled
their hand-embroidered sewing kits
their hedgehog pin-cushions. I marvelled

at the wonders they took out: lilliputian
scissors, silk-smooth darning eggs.
They kept up a twitter of self-deprecation

pecking at their dinner plates. Mother said
in the First World War they gave their food
rations to other girls at the Institute,

afterwards they measured four foot and a bit
were eighteen and never had a period.
At 12 I could look down on them but don't think I did.

Until they died in their late nineties
they donated all their savings to the poor, i.e.
an African village, my brothers and me

II

Under the roof in a two room flat lived
two elderly sisters, Irmela and Claire Foot.
Mother called them the Misses Feet.

They wore twenties style hairdos, pot-shaped hats
puce lipstick, rouge, kohl and they both
tied themselves up in whalebone corsets.

I was allowed see them in their underclothes.
Ample bosoms welled over satin bras,
feet a little swollen in high slingbacks

they taught me the dances of their youth
the fox-trot, tango, Charleston, jitterbug
said I was graceful on my feet.

Arbiters of feminine chic and proprieties
they embroidered my first party dress
laboriously with minuscule flowers.

On Sundays they would waltz off in their finery
and a cloud of Eau de Cologne to the five o'clock tea
dance with American soldiers at the Tivoli.

They'd been famous beauties long ago,
were engaged to two young officers
who both got killed in the Second World War.

No one was kinder or taught me more
than Aunt Elisabeth, Aunt Bella
Miss Irmela and Miss Claire.

INSTITUTE FOR HIGHER DAUGHTERS

I skulk in a corner as they step smartly
out of their clothes
kick off their petticoats
and slip into singlets and shorts.

Sometimes I feel their eyes slide over me
their amused looks, hear them whisper
as I pull my underdress over my head
ashamed of its lace trim.

This will do nicely till you're fourteen,
Mother said. *And just imagine*
your grandmother stitched
all that threadwork herself.

Bernadine's blond tresses sweep
the gymnasium floor
as she swings herself up
into the *Swan's Nest Position.*

They have an all-in music machine at home
mahogany with sliding doors
and a gentlemen's room where her father sits
smoking alone at night.

The gym teacher vows
she's a *primaballerina* on the rings whereas
I'm a sad failure on the horse nor
will I ever manage *Dead Man in the Pool.*

After class, as they dress and chatter, I envy
the ease with which they inhabit
their pale bulging flesh, their matter of fact tones
comparing cup sizes, love bites.

Words form on their lips and plop softly
like pink gum, exciting
and vaguely forbidden
lipstick, period, tampon, French kiss,

a sorority speaking a tongue
foreign to me, who's been sent
on Tuesdays from 2 to 4, the only girl
from the boys' school across the square.

At night I sit by the open window
overlooking the garden
the lilacs have just opened
and their scent lies heavy in the dark.

My pet snake has coiled itself around my arm,
bats are wildly fretting the tree tops.
I hear the car draw up, see its lights go out.
I eat strawberries, lick their juice from my fingers.

BREATHS AND VISIONS
Letter to Miriam, Galway, January 2003

"Breathe easy, breathe light, take short flat breaths",
the obstetrics student admonishes me again
pressing my shoulder deep into the mattress
till in one last exhalation of pain
a wave of scorching honey passes through me
or vice versa I through it
and you're eased out head and shoulders first
into the labour ward's echo and glare,
then, lifted, slapped, bathed, weighed
and measured, all in that order,
you catch your breath with a resounding cry,

(time-honoured hospital routine now replaced by
soft lighting, silent birthing-rooms and yoga
so when your baby's due next spring
I trust things clinical will be more comforting).

Light-headed with the oxygen I've inhaled
I laugh and tell the student that
in case he hadn't noticed there's no need
to hold me tethered any longer like a colt.
His face and uniform are dripping wet.

(The feeling of relief and joy's akin
to rising through the shadow-dark
of childhood lakes, banks bemired
with leaf mould, tadpole scum, tree bark
and plaited round with scotch grass, lady's
smock into the light of summer days,
emerging dizzy and buoyant
to catch a breath of air again).

Then after a near-swap with another child
(close shave) you're handed to me braceleted,
ID-ed and parcelled up in white
hospital issue cotton, and I fall
heart over heel for your small
creased matron's face,
the chick-down bloom on cheeks and skull,
the energetic chin just like my mother's,
the forehead of your father,
rounded, thoughtful,
the impish pert set of your mouth,
two hands, improbable and minuscule,
the pixie ears of the newborn. This one's yours,
the midwife comments, I should know,
and so you were, and I think are

still, some quarter century later,
next to you on a DGV speeding through
the sun-baked countryside of southern France,
and hardly daring breathe because
you lie stretched out across my lap,
summer-tanned, sporting a whole galaxy
of freckles, asleep in faded denims,
the canonicals of youth.
My delight is to the day as old as you
and tends to announce itself to all and sundry
like those biplanes curving round a July sky
streaming with rainbow-coloured tails
announcing circuses and festivals.

II

The eye — someone has said — is not a solver
of mathematical problems — true enough,
it is at times a chronicler of love

following on the heel of daughters
whose fingertips unleash *scherzos*
of creatures: kittens, budgerigars
terrapins, hamsters with elderberry eyes
and a sadly tedious nocturnal existence.
How can I say how complete a miracle she is
a Schubert song, a scent of C-major
a guide to fawn-legged deer
through lichen-frosted woods
out on sprees alike with seals and bats
and friends in threes and double scores.
When afternoons drop the monotone
letters of absence through the doors
and the traffic repeats its restless drone
it's then she appears in the vision house.

III

Remember us arriving late years ago
rushing from the underground into Heathrow?
you, togged out in Camden market shorts,
and I (both of us strange birds of sorts).
Hurried good-byes, you shoulder your rucksack
and vanish behind bullet-proof glass
a brief wave — thumbs up — behind the security check
in a delighted dumb-show of cutting loose.

Alone in the airport's sea roar,
no earthly use to you now, I imagine
you after take-off with nothing between
me — grounded here — and you except air,
seated now in the whispered ceremony,
the rituals of safety instructions,
you can still catch the odd glimpse of London
beneath its tattered white fleece as you fly

propelled past the clouds into ceiling-less blue,
and fight the panicked urge to head
for the Young Flyers' desk to do exactly — what?
Beg for a note to the pilot to steer you safely?
then remember what in the parting mêlée
(the rushed and tearful mock-heroics
of passport and ticket search, money, hugs)
I'd neither had the chance nor breath to say:

My dearest daughter in the skies,
among the ritual coffees and magazines,
look down at the earth
in its imaginary web of meridians:
take note of the islands, how the sea unrolls
bolts of cobalt blue cloth all around
as the pale trim of the coast appears,
observe the beautiful lie of the land,

the visionary yellows of rape fields,
villages scattered at random on green felt,
wide rivers flashing like mercury
winding through dusky terrains to the sea,
a city swings on a light-studded trapeze,
and lake-dappled, wood-studded plains
extend to mountains ranged like chorus lines,
and beyond them further to other seas.

Airborne at this height, put your faith
in the pilot but also in your young heart
to be your cartographer, to chart a course
that without doubt or shadow will be yours.
Come nightfall, take on trust the steady pulse
of wing lights, the good god Aeolus's
gift of fair winds, your trembling progress
on the downward spiral to your destined place.

IV

You've sent us per new-fangled electronic mail
two scanned images of what you call
"the sprogeen" that according to you
sometimes "wriggles about" ,
and other times is "totally conked out",
thumb in mouth, plus two thumbnail
sketches of its outline as visual aid for us,
who couldn't — forgive our fossil backwardness —
interpret the blurred print of the scan.
Your artist's training's never been
put to such use before, the digits plain
as daylight, the spinal chord and spine —
"you can see each single vertebra
like a necklace of beads", you say —
and the cranial curve, the exact volume
and fit for your still unexpanded womb,
fish-gilled and getting on swimmingly
in your waters. The unlikely wonder of it,
the likeness of your ante-natal portrait,
a flash of insight in the dark amniotic sea.

V

In one of your short videos
you allow us for a minute and a half or so
observe breath growing visible. Like all
inspired art it's elegant, unforced —
the camera focused on your mouth,
closed lips perfectly restful,
the background a light aqueous blue
conveying tranquillity, lull, dreams,
while imperceptibly the screen
mists over and the image bit by bit dissolves
in an all-enveloping shimmering haze.

It's the ultimate test in reverse –
the mirror held up to the mouth – not of the dead
this time but living. You have breathed
new life into the concept *spiritus.*
It makes me think of how we arrive
into the world fighting for breath
to say all that we think we need to say.
And yet on our walks to Gentian Hill
on stormy days the uncouth gusts will
pluck it from us flinging it across the bay.
(There seems to be so little weight in our words).
Let's celebrate instead your day of birth –
may Aeolus release the mild winds from his bag
for all your travels on your homeward trek,
(unless he's in the mood to commandeer a breeze
to play *divertimenti* in the trees).
Let's pray the formidable daughters of the night
will punctually arrive to play their part,
my dearest, when your baby's due next spring,
and may a glass or two of wine from Greece bring
roses to their ancient midwives' cheeks.

ARTIST IN HIS STUDIO

Wo Licht ist, ist Werden
Schelling

The oak panel leaning on the easel faces away from view –
a tilted upper case Alpha. As always
the beginning is shrouded in darkness.

Its shadow falls across sun-drenched floor boards
which are infiltrated by woodworm
writing the endless genesis of *anobium punctatum.*

The artist against the back wall is no more than 23
and no taller than an index finger,
dressed up, it appears, by travelling clowns

in silk, cambric and slouched velvet hat,
a proper dandy, were it not for the hobnailed boots
peering out from under his robe.

Only the tools of the trade: mortar and pestle,
plank table, palette on a hook,
instead of Persian carpets, fruit bowls from Delft,

no *mappa mundi* but outlines and faint marks
of unknown territories, river beds, caravan routes
on the discoloured whitewash.

A paint brush is poised like a surgical blade
about to make an incision in the heart of the world
in undying hunger for more world

on a canvas small enough to vanish inside my briefcase
together with panel, artist and brush —
the knife that dissects the shadow.

CREATIVE WRITING INSTRUCTIONS

Write bird
and hear it knock in the shell
watch spidery cracks appear on the page

write flight
as line after line
takes wing

write summer
and see elder blossoms
bewitch the June night

write dawn
and watch
the seven hues of grey awaken one by one

write morning
as the boy in the Esso station
dreams of the freeway

write river
and three dusty roads
will bring gossip from the coast

write window
and find it in the mutilated abbey
facing east beneath drapes of ivy

write young man
and across the city
a motorbike wakes from a chromium snooze

write jacket pocket
in which your hand
searches out your love's hand for warmth.

POETRY SEMINAR

Look. Here it is, a tent
under the flowering plum tree,
patched, leaky, with broken zip.

It's been here since August
or for the past five thousand years.
The maker's label has faded.
Spiders added their signatures.

It housed children once
an entire Arabian night of tales
starlight entered through the flap
ahead of the storyteller's long shadow.
Words followed and settled like obedient dogs.

You can live in it if you want —
dismantle it quickly, roll it up
and reassemble it wherever you like.
It will shelter you inside its blue grammar.
Each of its doors opens on silence.

If you listen well
it might tell you something familiar
that you never knew
not even in your wildest dreams.

Poems Found On A Strand
in Mannin Bay

for Leo Hallissey

I

Cells

On the coral strand near Shannanagower
I found a piece of what I thought
was washed-up Styrofoam –
it lay on my palm
white and weighing nothing at all
as though made of rice
paper, the merest breeze
could have blown it away –
roughly the size of a tennisball,
a little misshapen and subdivided
into multiple cells,
and I was told it was the egg case
of the common whelk.

But what is common about a creature
that hatches from such airy
and otherworldly honeycombs
and floats to the ocean ground
to grow itself a house with winding stair
and a whorl around the door,
the inside walls mother-of-pearl.

II

Purses

All the children searched the drift line
for mermaid's purses that afternoon,

inky, foursquare, antlered and tough
like a witch's uterus,
or oblong pouches with spiral-haired floats
made of taffeta, as though
dropped and forgotten by water sprites.

They clambered over rocks and beach
calling exultantly like the sedge-
warbler across the fields. The catch
of skate and dogfish flitting through the depths
was far beyond their reach.

III

Casings

A crab's casing, recently abandoned,
floats in the littoral surf.
Cannier than any other thing
on this strand, the crab
has just lifted the curve
of the lid and climbed
out of its own shell
and laterally sidled off.
I turn the armour, dark green buff
and dank as moss
with its limp appendices
of legs and shears, to gaze
at the gothic grimace
of its face. The dead eyes
on their stalks stare at me
as though crazed.

IV

Shells

We crossed over to Omey Island Indian file
through two fingers of water, half a mile
on the vast stretch of sand
between Omey and mainland.

Dogs and children racing ahead plus
the larks spinning out their *cavatinas*
provided an ambient island music
of twitter, dog bark, high melodic

cries, grass scent and pollen lay thick
in the air, a stonewall formed the backdrop
to some in-depth expert look
at flora, lichen, rock.

Within minutes we were prostrate
like Muslim penitents on our knees
to worship through magnifying glasses
the Persian miniature plants and grasses,

the densely woven prayer carpet
studded with the chalk-white shells
of the incumbent Omey snail:
lady's bedstraw, all bristling stalks

at give or take an inch and a half,
the *machair* fern, a lilliputian phallus,
between the cranebill's microscopic flowers
the scarlet pinheads of the pimpernel.

The larks played curtain-raisers all the while
to some bigwig herring gull's
dramatics in the aquatinted sky –
old hands at the annual summer show biz –

letting their highflown tautologies
tell you this world is all there is.

MAN ON BALCONY

A man is working out on a balcony   HOUSE?
stuck like a bit of black lace to the side of a hours
which looks down on the deserted lanes of an Italian town.

It is noon. Lunchtime ceremonials are enacted in every
                                        household
announced by the clattering of bowls and plates
the odd shout, laughter and the drone of midday chat
closing like a lazy tide above the tiled roofs.

The man on his balcony only wears gym shorts
and goes through a routine of knee-bends
push-ups, sit-ups, handstands.
Occasionally I see his head disappear
and two feet waver above the railing
like flesh-coloured pigeons about to take flight

then his gleaming torso snaps forward
or shoots round somersault-fashion
or, his arms flung open, he throws his head back
as if to call a blessing upon the masses
assembled in awed attendance on a distant square.

He looks like he's performing an oddly loose-limbed dance
or conducting the post-lunch concert
of motorbikes revving up
of high-pitched voices of schoolboys ascending
the hill to the People's Park for a soccer match.

He might be steeling himself, not so much to defy the earth
but, Atlas-like, to hold aloft for a while the white drifts
of cirrus and cumulus amassing above the town.
Perhaps he's training for the high wire act

next thing he'll fling a rope over to one of the castle towers
and stride out, free of ballast
infallible as a sky boy balancing the world on his chin
the soles of his feet pointing the way across the void
to anyone who cares to look up.

This man has taken up residence inside my head
since he appeared one rainy spring day in Urbino
slow motion gymnast on his balcony
turning and dancing above the roof tops as though
neither gravity were the issue nor the intolerable weight of the air
and I hope when he comes to the end
as he slides down to earth
that the rope will leave no burn marks in his palms.

BOY IN A GARDEN
Boston/Cambridge June 2003

for David Green

Some evenings are given to us as gifts –
how Boston that June, for instance, opened its heart valves
                                into the bay,
how the sweep of the Charles River divided the city
into a dark and a bright half,
how the arch of a bridge strung with lights
spanned the divide. I would choose a wide palette
of colours for this memory, from soft grey
to blue to a translucent inky blue running to black,
dusty greens for the squares and ivy-covered courtyards
we crossed on our way to the poetry reading,
opaque white for the little clapboard steeple
holding its golden tip aloft with such conviction.

We had been talking of war,
that in war time lies multiply and breed new lies
and words become worthless as inflationary coins,
but that we have no other weapon except language
to confront the counterfeit jargon of war,
its deathly rhetoric and the suppression of dissent
and that in our darkest moments we turn to poetry
for the consoling and illuminating word,
and as we entered the auditorium of the Meeting House
where the wall lamps were already lit
and cast amber waves over the barrel vault ceiling
we joined the other listeners seated on long benches

shifting closer together below whirring ventilator blades
as though ship-wrecked and rescued in this lumbering
over-heated ark, fanning ourselves with scraps of paper

49

till we resembled nothing more than a crowd of angels,
restless, fluttering, always on call.
A poet from Viet Nam said into the microphone:
>   *there in the peaceful church*
>   *I'd be a scholar, studious and frail.*
>   *I'd fall asleep with my head on a pile of books.*
The windows opened onto a garden where a young boy
had appeared on a bench, his white T-shirt faintly luminous
against the black dogwood trees.

In the hall another poet back from war spoke in simple words
of his loss and sorrow, his wounded memories.
The boy rose and walked around the garden,
sometimes standing still to raise his head and listen
with utmost concentration into the night.
As the poet made a plea for his young life to be returned to him
a death's head hawk moth flung itself
into the hall and started a mesmerised
tarantella back and forth from light to light
its shadow dancing aslant on the ceilings boards   *or ceiling's*
then as though recalled by a distant command
it tore itself loose and out.

My eyes were drawn to the boy, his aloneness,
his dream-like stance, and I wondered what he heard
and whether the pain and music of the lines would in time
raise a tree in his mind made of nightfall and tomorrow's
                                        flowering
and the syllabus of root and bud learned painstakingly by heart.
As we left the hall I saw the North Star had moved
a fraction closer to the steeple and I knew that in the distance
downtown Boston was a mirage of flickering neon,
but I also knew that this would stay with me always:

the poet, tired from study, resting his head on a cushion
                                    of words,
the other mourning his lost young life,
the visitor from the cave of shadows retreating,
the boy mysterious and solitary as Adam in the garden

OLD MAN IN AN ORCHARD

My unhappy children how long is the path,
until the destroyed garden may flower anew
Czeslaw Milosz

And old man, a poet, stands in his orchard
encircled by apple trees.
When he was nine, he and his family were exiled
to this country of mild fields and hedgerows.
The breeze ruffles his whit hair and the tolerant sun
scatters flecks of green light around his feet.
Each minute as the sandcliffs nearby dissolve
a little more in the Atlantic's onslaught,
so his memories of hate-crazed Berlin
are washed away by the salt flood of time.

He devoted much of his life to his orchard
each tree unfolded according to its own law and rhythm
in the certainty of seasons and cloud flight,
and to his poems, which to him
signified much the same labour
demanding the same careful attention,
nursing, and pruning and finally collection and reward.

For years he travelled the country in search of apples,
the out-of-favour ones in which aromas are stored
the world is forgetting (as it is forgetting
an entire vocabulary of tastes and must resort
to makeshift analogies – *cinnamon, berry, port,*
vanilla citron, quince –)
but no word was lost in the pure light of this garden:

Crow's Egg, Bellflower, Sweet Russet
Nonpareil, Leathercoat, Codlin
Black Hoover, Betsy Deaton, Bellflower
Permain, Catshead, Winesap,

Redstreak, Pomewater, Apple-John

Once when I visited him he was watching a beetle
streak past on green and golden wings.
Each tree was painted in the meticulous style of van Eyck
and filled with bird song,
the foliage close-knit and dark
which the painter had hung all over
with the round, glowing lanterns of apples.

His face in the shadow of leaves
was like one of the faces you sometimes find
in old country churches
so high up you can hardly see them
looking down from between the ribs
of the sky-carrying vault.

Mist in June Near Carrig na mBan

or

Zen Mountaineers Prefer to Climb Mount Fuji in the Fog

It was only when I reached the age of 73
that I began to grasp the true form and nature of birds,
fishes and plants. By the time I am 80 I will have made
some more progress. At the age of 90 I will comprehend
the essence of all things. At 100 I will reach a high degree
of perfection and if I live to be 110, everything I create,
every stroke and dot, will live. Hokusai

Last night a mist came inland from the sea,
dragged layers of heavy sodden felt
across the Twelve Bens and the bay,
and wielding a large soft brush
it primed the world with a grey wash.

The wind which usually runs full tilt
is hung up like a slack old coat,
and the blue ships beside the pier
lie half turned over on their sides
as in a dream, their tangled nets

are filled with broken stars and shears.
Just yesterday the world was definite and clear
but now all lines seem vague and blurred.
Even the cuckoo that wakes us at dawn
ex cathedra surveying her domain

from an electric pole outside the house
counts out our few remaining years
with slightly dampened confidence.
If you are wandering on days like this
go into one of the luminous fields,

54

where colours show themselves up close
to you, spreading in concentric rings
around three peaceable white cows
lowering their soft-muzzled heads
to the abundance of wet grass.

Flag irises stand tall among the reeds,
their raincoat-yellow pointed hoods rolled tight
or loosely bunched up round their throats,
lording it over fog-drenched buttercup and daisy
bee orchid, lady's smock and meadow rue.

Lie back letting a winged shadow pass
you overhead, then turn and read the grass,
its varied, unspectacular script
of roots and pollen, panicles, and seeds
like downy tufts on old men's heads,

and note on every blade and freshened leaf
the droplets gather pulling them to earth
rolling like water from a bird,
the wires of fences strung with spheres
that transport each an upturned universe.

The mist will serve you on a shimmering plate
the inside story, the more intimate view
of things the sweeping dramas hide from us,
something the artists of the Mustard Seed
Garden School of painting knew

precisely painting mosses dot by dot
with concentration and their minds at peace.
The cuckoo's got the last word noon and night,
her lovely repetitions carry weight:
Don't fret, she says, what's true is true.

THE LATITUDE OF NAPLES

For Eoin

I

With this pen as my eidograph
I draw the map,
the ground plan of power
and the street plan of destruction:

first the central square
with the ducal palace – or what's left of it,
the fountain doubling as pillory
(the irony of the life-giving well
beside the neck irons of scorn),

then the North Eastern road
leading across the New Bridge –
now out of service –
from which you can see Black Island
with the Lepers' Tower,
straight to St Andrew's Fortress.

I sketch the arsenal with its tall oak gates
and tiny apertures high up in the South wall.
The river loops around the old city castle
19 times ransacked and now in ruins
however, underground passages and casemates
might still have some use.

The wall existed not so much
to protect the inhabitants
but to prevent them
from exiting without a pass.

The only gate, the Gate of Persuasion,

is surmounted with a fine tympanum
depicting the rhetorical arts in marble.

Maybe they talked themselves to death inside
once the gate was locked forever
and no one came out or went in.

I draw the avenue from the ducal palace
to the citadel overlooking the city
(which is even more fortified
than many of the municipal buildings),

then the two graveyards –
once strictly segregated according to religion –
with their countless tombstones
and blackened inscriptions
and last of all taking special care
I draw a swallow's nest with five nestlings
under the eaves of the gravedigger's hut.

II

The first time you brought me
to your room
we were islanded
on your coral bed

lying in each others' arms
in the ear of the night
on tidal waves of jazz
and street noise

dreaming of bays
interlaced with rigging and masts
till the sun rose, bakers in white
mounted their bikes all over the city

and a clear pathway led
as far as the latitude of Naples
and along the old silk road
to Samarkand

III

There it is / closed now/
had wings once / sang
caused trouble / lived overground
built nests / swore / lied
stone heavy / stone rich /stone hard
fit into a hand once / had fingers once
held one just like it / had seeds once
seeds like moons / seeds and words
words and syntax / bone language / wing language
not now / shut down / and shuttered
had light once / saw
had sound once / heard
lies still now / stone deaf /stone blind

IV

Since the musicians moved in
love was declared in our street
turtledoves appeared in the trees
Debbie put on her dancing shoes
the heron returned from out of town
sailed in with blue sails.

V

No matter where we went
you read the cities
in the palm of your hand.

58

With you I trusted again
in the tortuous paths
through iron gardens

and temples whose roots
grew from reptile cages.
One look at the map

and you knew your way
between silk routes
and golden gates.

You sent word from Ninive   *Niniveh ?*
where the light
lay imprisoned between yew trees.

Below ghetto walls
when darkness erupted
you brought me hot mutton soup.

Salt winds and Spain
lay like a beating red heart
in an ultramarine bowl.

Persia, a prayer rug spread over a desert
crossed by the nonchalant stride
of the camel.

Near Ararat we threw driftwood
into the iron stove, warmed ourselves
with waterpipe smoke.

We followed the 53 stations
of the East Sea Road
and it was still raining in Shonu.

Worlds travelled through us,
you took me downtown at night to music
played on blue keyboards.

WASHING MY MOTHER

I

Grass grow over me
bridge let me fall
cloud come and hide me –
my mother's long hair
was cut off by nurses
too busy to brush it.

Vein flow for me
heart pump for me
eye close for me –
they stabbed their scalpels
into my mother's spinal cord.

Door dismiss me
syringe stitch an exit for me
stairs be my catapult
mortuary shine with your tiles for me –
they didn't give my mother the time
so she could say goodbye.

Herr Doktor, pronounce your judgement.
Frau Doktor, take half the pain.
Fräulein Schwester, share out the sorrow.

II

Mother of quince
mother of rosehips
mother of sweet pockets
mother of narrow gauge railway timetables
mother of starch and cambric

61

mother of Bohemian winds
mother of algebra
mother of bicycles
mother of hypotenuses
mother of sonatinas
mother of clove, feather and milk
mother of Greek syntax
mother of buttercups
mother of winter trams
mother of rivermeadows
mother of camomile
mother of yeastcakes
mother of original mildness
mother of blue crockery
mother of the final house

III

When she died,
the mountains
lakes, forests around her house,
the fuchsia bushes
she had tended, all went silent
and the lampshades
filled with butterfly husks.

The last imprint of her fingers
on her soap –

the last imprint of her head
on her pillow –

Through the windows
darkness flooded the room,
the morning came to her bed too late.
The world had been adjourned.

IV

After I'd undressed her
she lay before me like a child,
without shame, her body still and bare.
I'd never seen her naked before
and was full of fear.
There was a basin of warm water
so nothing cold would touch her
and a bar of her special scented soap.
Outside the summer ran
through one artful colour
scheme after another.
The hills lay calm and blue
in the late afternoon light
and a breeze through the window
fingered and brushed the curtains aside.
A slip of a day moon idled slowly by.
I washed her then, her silent face,
lifting the strands of hair
the busy nurses had cut short,
her neck, her throat,
I washed the ribbed vault of her chest,
flat as a young girl's,
her shrunken breasts.
She was so thin
the bones showed singly
underneath the skin.
I'd never known she'd wasted so away.
Where did I have my eyes?
How did she manage to disguise
this so well? I touched
where a fracture'd mended
badly in her collar bone,
the white seam of a scar.
I washed her stomach,

the navel's recess, her pelvis,
its generous shallow bowl. I felt
her skin smooth as suede,
rosewood, cool as water, crinkled
and fine as crêpe de chine.
I washed with reverence
the gentle rise
of her pubis, her sex now hairless
washed her secret flesh,
her gaunt flanks and thighs.

We had changed places, she and I.
For the first time I did
for her what without question
she had often done for me.
And yet despite her silence she
commanded everything, still taught
me as she once had about life
all that she knew of death.
Her eyes lay deep below
their rounded lids.
Her mouth was soft and calm.
I dressed her then, the air was warm
and summer evening blue.

THE LAST HOUSE
afte Rainer Maria Rilke

No matter who you are, when evening comes
get up and leave your room with the familiar
things, scattered books, photographs
pinned to the shelves,
no matter who you are.

And as you step outside into a lively scene
of buildings, people, traffic rushing past,
it strikes you that your house is last
before the empty distances begin,

and though you're tired beyond words,
your eyes too tired to lift themselves across
the busy threshold of your house,
yet they will slowly raise aloft a tree   see p. 50
and place it standing straight against the sky,
black, slim and solitary,

and you have made the world anew,
and it is vast and silent,
a word picked early as a fruit
that's left to ripen in the sun.

But at the moment when
you think you've understood
what it all means, your eyes
let go of it again with tenderness.

ROZHINKES MIT MANDLEN

I wanted at least to preserve their faces.
Roman Vishniak, photographer

Yidele, Motl, Avrem,
Yankele, Tsipele, Sarah,
where did they take you?

***

Aunt Fini wears her pearl earings
she sits at the head of the table.
Next to her Uncle Moishe,
then Aron, then Mother
and on the other side my cousin the beautiful Sarah
with her arm around me.
We don't look at the camera because
it is the Seder evening
we are hungry
and there is fish soup in the pot.
The tin mug hanging on a nail
behind Aunt Fini was my father's
but he's gone I don't know where.

***

On the steps to the shop
two best friends –
pig tails and blond curls
a ragged woollen coat
a dirty pinafore –
sharing lemon drops
in the July heat

***

My father is a locksmith
and works at home.
When he fixes a lock
he wears his working cap
and I wear mine
because I help him
all the time.

We have two beds
with carved crests
standing in our room,
one for the six children
one for Dad and Mum.

***

On Sabbath I wear
my coat with the fur collar
and two buttons
as big as a five crown piece,
my brother Joshele has brushed his locks,
he carries the holy book.

***

One – nut – empty
two – twins – gone
three – coins – spent
four – wheels – broken
five – fingers – burnt
six – children – gassed
seven – gathered – lost
eight – think straight – wept
nine – degrees – froze
ten – seeing men – killed
eleven – a body – hurt

twelve – a clock – stopped
thirteen – whips - lashed
fourteen – stitches – cut
fifteen – years – died

***

Only Motl has shoes
so he must be the horse
Yossi holds the reins
and I hold Yossi's hand.

***

Grandmother knows the best stories
how the angel came to Tobias
how Lot's wife turned to salt
and how the sheaves of wheat
standing in a circle bowed to Joseph.
When she holds me in her arm
and calls me her *maedele*
I feel so good and warm.

***

My father is a shoemaker
his name is Adam Mandelbaum.
My mother's called Mirjam Mandelbaum
and I am Felix Mandelbaum.
The almond tree is the most beautiful tree.
I saw one once in a garden in Lodz.
I am six years old
I like to sing
and eat raisins and almonds.

FROM SALOME OF LURIA'S LEXICON OF HERBS, SPICES AND CURES

O Lychorida, bid Nestor bring me spices, ink and paper.
Shakespeare, Pericles, Prince of Tyre, III,1

Indeed, Sir, she was the sweet marjoram of the salad, or rather
the herb of grace
Shakespeare, All's Well That Ends Well, IV, 5

Arrowroot

An envelope arrived today by post
from the Americas
containing a powder which
when mixed with red wine from Castile
will make a poultice to draw the poison
from any love-
wounded heart

Basil

In groups of two, three, a dozen
happiness leaves
they lodge in the spring garden
mothers of seven
below the roof of my mouth
love's lettuce
searching for the taste of truth
king's wort
with fragrant fingertips.

Caraway

Intoxicant of northlands,
sickle moon in forests crossed
and recrossed by thirsty reindeer herds
on the way to the cisterns of knowledge.

Cardamom

Black grains crushed between my teeth,
the eye in the needle of flavour
opens wide –
enter and tongue the bright mouth.

Coriander

I remember a thoroughbred outside every house
in the village of Wadi Musa,
high-spirited, pawing the ground,
men in a circle on the square
shared hummus and bread,
towards evening dry golden seeds of manna rained
from the minarets.

Cloves

I've planted a myrtle tree for each child
and if it flourishes
the child will prosper.
From the bark I extracted
a brown liqueur to sweeten the verse
recited by my court versifier
into his empress' ear.

Dill

My hand secure in the warmth
of grandmother's hand,
her hat-feather nodding.
Dilla, dilla – lullaby in high summer,
refrain from the days of cornflower paths,
grass song of rabbit's bread,
love-grass, woman's hair, shiver grass.

Fennel

Umbellate blossoms, bloodbespattered,
trampled into the ground
as far as the eye can see –
the Battle of Marathon was fought
on a golden field.
The warriors' souls
have shed their bodies
and are eating fennel seeds
to restore their vision.

Ginger

She lives somewhere in the city,
lost child of the streets,
undertone of pop songs,
unruly heckler spicing our disputes
in coffee houses
with her zing.

Juniper

Bitter scent wafts from oracle caves.
The black candle wicks
of prophecy burn.

71

I watch my step
on singed ground.

Mustard Seeds

Breaking free of the dark earth
they float towards me
incomparable, munificent,
tiny boats bearing green sails.

Nutmeg

I have pounded *myristica fragrans* in the mortar
and ground it into a fine powder but
there's no knowing what will happen
if I administer this to you, my sick lover,
together with attar of roses
and hot white wine –
which fevers will I quench
and which rekindle?

Parsley

Harvested on riverbank allotments
petroselium – a crisp green froth
which I wind round my sweetheart's neck
to keep foul fumes from harming him.
But if he ever cheats on me
I'll pick a sprig and say his name
and he will perish miserably.

Rosemary

Small flowers recall
the feathery weight of a cloak
casually draped over this aromatic bush.

So earnest, loving and loyal,
aflame with longing,
blue incense rising from bare rock.

Saffron

One breath is enough,
bright between my fingertips,
reverie in the earliest meadows
of the year.
Yellow of such purity
must have been salvaged
from deep beneath the winter grass.

Sage

The goddess enchanted by the perfumes
of her spring garden quite forgot
to fill Persephone's pockets
with the silvery leaves
of *salvia,* the mother herb
which would protect her from the bite of snakes
so she was bitten and then carried off to Demeter's wild grief
by the pale master of the underworld.
I chop sage into every dish, my love,
to give you strength of mind and body
and to keep you safe.

Salt

This old language
came from a distant country
and sailed on the back of a river
directly towards two goats
standing beside the water
in a field rampant with ferns and brambles,

their coat's weave
of white and pewter threads
luminous among the various greens.

Star Anise

Children of the stars
wooden rosettes
turning their minute mill wheels
on the lip of mildness.

Sugar

Crystals that whisper
rub against each other and melt
in reflections of glittering islands.
How dark the world seems tonight
seen in their light.

Sumac

In the bazaar at Aleppo
I hawk the sour fruit of the vinegar tree
to fat merchants from Tripoli and Alexandria
to tickle their palates,
their insatiable appetites.

I dance for them
on the steps to the ziggurat
in sumac yellow, in zaffre blue silk
till they shower me with gold.

In the dark alleys of Jerusalem
I cure them of their pox
with pills which I've prepared
from poison tree and balsam fir

one scruple each of exudation of berries and resin
mixed with powdered pokeroot –
not easy to come by these days –
a talent of silver a piece.

Tarragon

Grey Moorish silk,
leaf-embroidered tent-roof
of gentle-spoken nomads.
Iridescent fish
sprung from mosaic walls.

Za'attar

In a garden that sloped down to the sea
I stilled the hungers of my childhood
beneath olive and citrus trees
with freshly baked bread spread with Za'attar
broken and passed around from one to another
savour and spice unfolding
their musical scales on my tongue

SONATA OF THE PAINTER'S SHADOW

I

INTRODUCTION
Allegro assai

He painted the first one in red,
the sky was a loom above the sea,
countless shuttles ran to and fro weaving the sunset.

For the second and third ones he chose blue,
two ancient sisters knitted peacocks in the suburbs,
the air was silk shot through with kingfishers.

The next four flourished in green,
cross stitch of grass sleeves, pearl stitch of seaweed collar,
zigzag of the undertow, buttonhole of morning seas.

Eight appeared in violet black,
ten cuttlefish spun a mantilla of ink,
the night reeled the new moon in on its spool.

Sixteen were splendid in yellow,
honey hum carpeted the village, Chinese lanterns
made from the plush of wasps hung in the trees.

Thirty-two wore white
and the world turned young with patterns of clouds.
The wind worked the treadle of a whitewashed house.

II

CHORUS OF OLD MEN
Andante maestoso con moto

It must be because the Great Mother has no arms
that her daughters don't either,
so they tamed the bull and made a pet of the pig
and where does that leave us?

And because the Great Mother has no legs to speak of
her daughters don't either,
seated on the crescent moon in their nest-of-snakes head-dresses
they tell us to stop moaning.

As for eyes and ears, who needs them
if they can relax their cheekbones
with an iceblue swiveldrink
laughing at our distress

in a furry recess of the grotto
where the swells
crash over the rocks washing their fall-out
into the world like milk?

III

CHORUS OF THE GIRLS
Allegretto ma non troppo e molto cantabile

after Alkman

Lucky who gets through the day without crying.
I'm under Deirdre's spell, she is prettier than a model.
But our famous choir-mistress is jealous
and forbids me all praise or criticism of Deirdre

since she herself shines like a thoroughbred
among cattle, accustomed to winning whoever she wants.
She's an apparition in dreams
dreamt in shadows below the cliffs of Achill.

You can see her, can't you? A pure-blooded Arabian racer!
My cousin Emer's locks grow and blossom
in waves of pale yellow and her face shimmers like silver –
why should I describe her to you in detail? There she is herself!
Only Deirdre could equal her beauty.
It's a toss-up between the horses of Connemara and Donegal.
The Seven Sisters rise followed by the Hound of Orion
and compete with us as soon as we deliver
the morning veil to the goddess.

We don't have enough red silk for the coming onslaught
nor gold bracelets winding around our arms like snakes
nor Spanish turbans, head-dress for delicately mascaraed girls,
nor Gráinne's plentiful hair, there is neither a sign of Medhb,
the striking beauty, nor Aoife or Eithne,
and I have no intention to go up to Niamh
and ask her: "Could I have Orla,
and would you ask Róisín or the lovely Nuala
with her rhinestone hairslides to take a good look at me?"
because Emer keeps me under strict surveillance.

Where is Deirdre the girl with long white feet?
She does hang around Fiona and praise the meals
I am preparing. Hear the prayers of those two,
immortal goddess! Because success and purpose
are in your hands I now gather courage to ask:
Mistress of the choir, I am only a girl
and like a small owl on barn rafters, I screech
lighthearted into the blue –
but I want to ask you for the gentle protection of Bríd,
because she assists us during intolerable birth pains.

Thanks to Deirdre's efforts, we girls won the battle
and are enjoying peace, hard-won it was, too,
from hard-headed men, followers of the ludicrous god
who loves bloodshed and war. We
ignore them as well as we can –
their gargoyle faces convulsed with self-pity
are not a pretty sight.
Let them congregate in the desert of Aran and sacrifice
to their missile-headed deity as much as they like.

Alright, so Emer's not as good as the Spice girls
but in the choir of eleven she sings as loud as ten
and her voice resounds like the song of the gull
on the fast-flowing currents of the Shannon.

IV

CHORUS OF MEN GIVING SEASONAL ADVICE TO POLYGAMOS
Scherzando vivace

After Alkaios

1.
When rain falls in icy torrents
and northerlies rage over Ireland

kindle the flames in the grate
mix wine in the jug with muscat

and free of care lay your block-
head on a cushy woolsack.

Turn off TV, computer, mobile, leave bills
and papers on the floor in the hall.

Why get heated about women or corruption
if you can drink your way into oblivion.

79

Put a wreath of dill stalks
for their scent round your neck,

and rub sweet almond oil on your chest.
To stop girls from disturbing your rest

place crushed berries of the bitter juniper
across the threshold of your door.

2.
When the Dog Star makes its round at night
and the world lies dead in the fiery heat

when cicadas weave spells in tops of trees
when artichokes bloom, and drugged bees

sleep in blossoms like poisoned phials   (vials?)
when women are beside themselves

with desire, men grow soft in their purpose
(heads and knees dried out by Sirius),

then wet your insides, reach for the glass
the rainbow coloured one you often use.

Why wait for the light?
The day is no more than two fingers wide.

Mix two potent ones for you and me,
to keep thoughts of the sisterhood at bay.

Here's to us lads, lift your
fragrant brimful snifter.

V

FINALE – CODA

My sisters and I watch the painter's hand
and the long shadow of his arm
move crabways across the canvas
its heat brushing against us like the words
noir d'ivoire.
cadmium orange
coeruleum.   *(cerulean ?)*

We emerge from the surge of the undercoat
so fast our bodies can hardly keep up
with the fingers holding the charcoal
scrabbling dark and rodent-like
across the surface of light
chalkwhite
giallo di Napoli
woad.

Before this my sisters and I were ordinary women
with ordinary longings, fell in love, had children,
took them to the blue doors of the water,
the green gates of the forest, sang
windblown songs of tall ships to them,
the melodies of the yellow buckwheat
ultramar   *(ultramarine)*
magenta
tierra verde.   *(terra verde ?)*

But the painter's pact with the shadowy old faces
each in a rictus of rage or dismay
growing from the tight urns of our wombs
Payne's gray
raw umber

condemns us to this glacial world
in which we are fixed and stretched
like fine white chamois
or spread around, red as old blood
and as silken to the touch
madder
flesh
jaune citron

and already we are forgetting the beginnings:
our mother, midnight, warmth, disorder,
our midwifery skills and instruments,
the time when no one dared hover godlike over the waters
commandeering the moon
forcing us into the light
Vandyke brown
rojo Indio   *(rocho?)*
bitumen.

THE READER

Daily I read the blue novel of the sky,
turning page after page,
I follow the dazzling protagonist
on a difficult and solitary journey.

At night the narrative changes
as the dark theatre fills
with countless characters: stand-up comedians,
ferrymen, nymphs, hunters,

a whole zoo of bears, whales, unicorns,
and even objects, rusty
old shields, crowns,
weighing scales, belts.

At the centre of the action
the coolest of players
bathing in the light
of reflected glory.

The clouds have long chapters
devoted to them
in which their short tempers
and tendency to erupt,

their birth in rivers and lakes
and their hopeless love
for the light
are discussed in detail,

also the 15-odd different shades of dawn
its morning chat
with the early risers, the birds
are minutely recorded.

Many pages of this novel are torn
and dog-eared
from generations of readers,
and rain has discoloured its jacket

which tends to slip from the binding,
but the blurb still states majestically
that it is the highlight
of this particular author's oeuvre,

the true *magnum opus*,
not a facsimile but the real McCoy,
whose fans run into numbers
inexpressible to the nth degree.

SURVIVORS

We are God's memory
Elie Wiesel

We're back from nowhere
after an eternal absence.
Part of us is still there circling
the dark wastes.

Being God's memory is too much of a burden,
unvolunteered for.
The revolving doors had chanced
to deposit us on this side of life,

(coincidence or a guilty betrayal
of fate) and here we are in the glare
of a street lamp or on a park bench
together with our unpronounceable past

for which even the folds of our coats
our neatly draped scarves
and humble gloves and hats
seem to apologise.

Paperwork, regulations, signatures,
A raised voice, the slam of a door –
too much of this and we might fall
apart, spill over onto the pavement

into the extrasystolar pounding
of traffic, the noise that settles
on unfamiliar places
like ashes.

Be gentle with us –
we know the doctors of death
forget nothing or no one
and neither the light hoisting its sail

through the blue glittering wash
nor the golden mosaic face
of mercy
are turned towards us.

SEQUELS

Past title, jacket blurb and foreword,
halfway through the most uneventful first
twenty-eight pages it dawns on us

that we are caught in a sequel
and what happened in Part I
will never be quite revealed.

Perhaps it was full of drama
war, sacrifice, intrigue?
We, however, trapped in the inferior present

try to remember
how on earth we got here, on what road
leading down which mountains, and why.

Sometimes we wish someone would
rip out our chapter
where nothing ever happens

not a single proposal, no elopements,
not even the tiniest betrayal,
just silent weeks after measles

in a room with a patchwork rug
where the *plink plink* of a piano
being tuned below can be heard

and we wake to musical scales
running up and down like stairs
to the same empty hallways.

The exciting part of the plot
must have already occurred
or is reserved for the future

which we hope to watch from the wings
of our sickbeds
if Doctor P. allows:

The lovers will be back
without signs of ageing,
no wrinkles, not one grey hair.

She still wears the choker with the cameo
Count C. gave her,
and tours the garden with Frederick

or was it Arthur, who entered
through the French doors,
climbed the stairs, left a billet-doux.

Once more the enactment of jealousies,
tinkling pianos and fizzy refreshments
gardeners delivering freesias or raspberries.

But since sequels offer variations,
however slight,
there's hope that the scene

in the music room of the sanatorium,
between H. and Madame Ch. for instance,
will - given the chance - not be repeated:

the glove won't be stripped off the identical hand
and its attendant palm kissed
by exactly the same moustachioed lips

the pharmacist will run out of laudanum
the duellists misfire
the late train will be diverted to another station.

Where solutions precede problems
recovery the illness,
we are dizzy with possibilities:

We will send off that letter
and it won't slip down behind the box
and into oblivion.

Doctor P.'s prognosis will be optimistic,
we will make that phone call
and turn up in time for the rendezvous

which we will walk out of after delivering
the most cracking punch line,
we will count our victories and also our losses.

We could begin again because after all
sequels are just another beginning.
We could even take a look at the misty hills

visible for the first time in years,
where the past cascades down
like a shimmering ribbon.

SHOES

For Adrian and Clíodhna

Older than his country, almost
as old as the century,
a man who has given himself to the harsh
labour of dying never notices the years
falling away one by one or the rain feeding
the moss on his roof
nor the grey static of snow falling
on his TV screen nor the stains spreading across the plaster
where he lies inside the dusty halo of a 40 Watt bulb.

A light has settled on his face during the last seconds
round mouth and eyes, of relief or irony maybe, and the nun
who finds him next day is struck
by his expression, and while his meal grows cold
inside the foil, she stands and wonders what
his last laugh may have been about.

He's stretched out in his Sunday best as though
he had expected some momentous caller,
and the feet she's come to know better
than her own with their hard
brown curving nails she used to soak
for an hour before she could make any
headway with the clippers
are still encased in shoes, black and coffin-like
casting stiff shadows on the wall.

They remind her of a story she'd read long ago,
years before the convent,
of Iris, messenger of the gods,
who never took her shoes off
even during sleep so she'd be ready always

to deliver messages from the Olympians
to the mortals on earth without delay,

and how odd it is, muses the nun,
walking from room to room,
that all he's leaving to his unknown heirs
in Perth or Philadelphia are this derelict house
and a multitude, a convention of shoes,
living their strange double lives
wherever she looks, on armchairs, shelves,
piled on the kitchen table even,
dozens of pairs, open-laced,
with lolling tongues and glinting
nails, hooks and eyes
resting like tired beasts of prey:

marching, fighting, prison shoes,
walking on air, keeping in step
stepping it out, falling in
and out of love shoes,
shoes for the endless trot,
the slippery parquet, the office floor,
happier people's wedding parties,
treadmill, disillusionment, redundancy,
bus shelter shoes,
off-licence, sister-burial
rage, loneliness, despair shoes,
no more voting for liars, afraid of hospital
not understanding the world
refusing to take the medication
not giving a damn anymore shoes.

Shoes with wings, with watermarks,
with light step and heavy soles
and finally shoes fit for a mortal
to take a pithy message to the gods.

REQUIEM ON FATHERS' DAY, BOSTON 2001

(i.m. Michael Patrick Quinn,
May 27, 1946 - August 29, 1969)

When I arrived by air I found no borders
no borderlines to cross a single word –
the ocean-going city took me in

as peace talks were in progress everywhere
the air breathed promises of armistice to all
and sundry underneath catalpa trees

that stood in tattered white like Mrs Havishams
and where the hanging tree had been
young fathers bathed their offspring in the wading pool.

This was the hour of fathers in the park
and they marched in *to make a difference*
in their hundreds. The undivided city

took me as a laugh and two young men
certified me fit company
for www.swanenterprise.com.

In *parks on wheels* without frontiers
I stole a handkerchief of shade
a pocketful of earth and slept

beneath the awning of a tree.
A saxophone broke the afternoon's heart
and wept until the evening came round.

It wept for Michael Patrick Quinn
"a Latin graduate from Boston"
who worked the Swan Boats in the summer

and died in action at the age of 23
far in the distant land of Viet Nam.
His name was written on the bridge

where waterbirds build nests on stilts
and squirrels share the secret ownership
of this high-flying garden

with the homeless only, who are residents
of lost uproarious nights in June.
When fledglings fell like rain

through the mimosa tops, a troupe
of woe-begones in tee-shirts
called my eye to cardio vascular disease. My heart

lay open on a bench in light of trees
lay still and listened to the song
played by a solitary saxophone

for young Lieutenant Michael Patrick Quinn.

ZEUS IN SUBURBIA

And suddenly our relaxed talk
of humus and pest control
of how to shelter saplings broke

off – three women at a table laden with odds
and ends, seed packets, secateurs,
for just outside the glass doors

to the garden a swan stood
lost in the tangle and foliage of mid-
summer, startling and white

the musical wings folded tight
around himself, his short
black-stockinged legs apart

on splayed feet flat as trowels
swivelling his carneval's
mask face to and fro to peer at us

then withdrew, web-toed and marvellous,
lumbered across a bed of blue iris
and trapped in the rank growth

in the back he sank down among tall weeds,
his blasé-looking head afloat for hours,
a dandy's flower above the dandelion flowers

As the day's green wheel rotated
slowly we sat silent, light as birds. Late
we opened the back door to night

and canal water latitude. For weeks we'd still
find grass and daisies crushed
the odd stiff shimmering quill.

Notes:

In Praise of Round Things

Miles van der Rohe, 1886-1969, German architect and director of Bauhaus.

Osias Beert, 17th century Flemish painter.

Orrery of the Great Earl, mechanical device showing the movement of the planets around the sun which is named after Charles, Earl of Orrery.

Willendorf Venus, prehistoric fertility goddess found near Willendorf, Austria.

"pond in the forest" refers to the Blaue Topf, a small lake of intense blue near Blaubeuren in Southern Germany; according to folk-legend it is inhabited by a nymph of the same blue.

Parmigianino, 16th century Italian painter from Parma; his self-portrait is in the kunsthistorische Museum in Vienna.

Landscapes with Figures

"the young Swiss writer", Peter Weber, from Wattwil, Toggenburg, author of "Der Wettermacher".

Little Island

Both "Little Island" and "Place of Drunkenness" are Native American names for Manhattan.

Rozhinkes mit Mandlen

Yiddish children's song; the poem is based on Roman Vishniak's book of photographs of the 1930s taken in the stetls of Poland, entitled "Children of a Lost World."

96